INDIANA DUNES
NATIONAL PARK
ACTIVITY BOOK

PUZZLES, MAZES, GAMES, AND MORE ABOUT
INDIANA DUNES NATIONAL PARK

NATIONAL PARKS ACTIVITIES SERIES

INDIANA DUNES NATIONAL PARK ACTIVITY BOOK

LITTLE BISON

Press

For more free national parks activities, visit
Littlebisonpress.com

About Indiana Dunes National Park

Indiana Dunes National Park is located in the state of Indiana. The park was elevated from National Lakeshore to National Park in 2019.

This park covers 15,000 acres of sand dunes, wetlands, prairies, forests and covers 25 miles of Lake Michigan shoreline. It is the fifth most biodiverse national park in the United States! Indiana Dunes is known as the birthplace of the science of ecology (the study of organisms and how they relate to one another and their physical surroundings).

There are lots of historic structures visitors can explore, including National Historic Landmarks. The Bailly Homestead was the home of Honore Gratien Joseph Bailly de Messein (1774 - 1835). Bailly was a historic figure that played a role in the development of northern Indiana.

Indiana Dunes National Park is **famous for:**
- the unique environment and diverse ecology
- 15,000 acres of dunes, wetlands, prairies, and old-growth forests
- 50 miles of trails
- historic sites and structures

Hey! I'm Parker!

I'm the only snail in history to visit every National Park in the United States! Come join me on my adventures in Indiana Dunes National Park.

Throughout this book, we will learn about the history of the park, the animals and plants that live here, and things to do here if you ever get to visit in person. This book is also full of games and activities!

Last but not least, I am hidden 9 times on different pages. See how many times you can find me. This page doesn't count!

Bird Scavenger Hunt

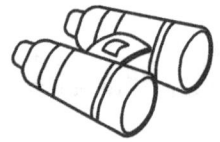

Indiana Dunes National Park is a great place to go birdwatching. You don't have to be able to identify different species of birds in order to have fun. Open your eyes and tune in your ears. Check off as many birds on this list as you can.

☐ A colorful bird   ☐ A big bird

☐ A brown bird   ☐ A small bird

☐ A bird in a tree   ☐ A hopping bird

☐ A bird with long tail feathers   ☐ A flying bird

☐ A bird making noise   ☐ A bird's nest

☐ A bird eating or hunting   ☐ A bird's footprint on the ground

☐ A bird with spots   ☐ A bird in the water

What was the easiest bird on the list to find? What was the hardest?
Why do you think that was?

_____

_____

Snail Mail

Design a postcard to send to a friend or a family member. Who do you want to tell about Indiana Dunes National Park? In the first template, write your message. In the second template, create a design for the front of the postcard. You could show something you saw, something you did, or something you want to do in the national park.

Postcard

Things to Do Jumble

Unscramble the letters to uncover activities you can do while in Indiana National Park. Hint: each one ends in -ing.

1. BOTA
   ☐☐☐☐ING

2. KIH
   ☐☐☐ING

3. IRDB
   ☐☐☐☐ING

4. MACP
   ☐☐☐☐ING

5. KINICPC
   ☐☐☐☐☐☐☐ING

6. EISSTEHG
   ☐☐☐☐☐☐☐☐ING

7. SARTGZA
   ☐☐☐☐☐☐☐ING

Word Bank

birding
reading
camping
stargazing
boating
hiking
hunting
singing
yelling
sightseeing
picnicking

6

Build a Bird Nest

Different birds build different kinds of nests where they can lay their eggs and raise their babies.

Draw a nest and some baby birds that you might find in Indiana Dunes National Park.

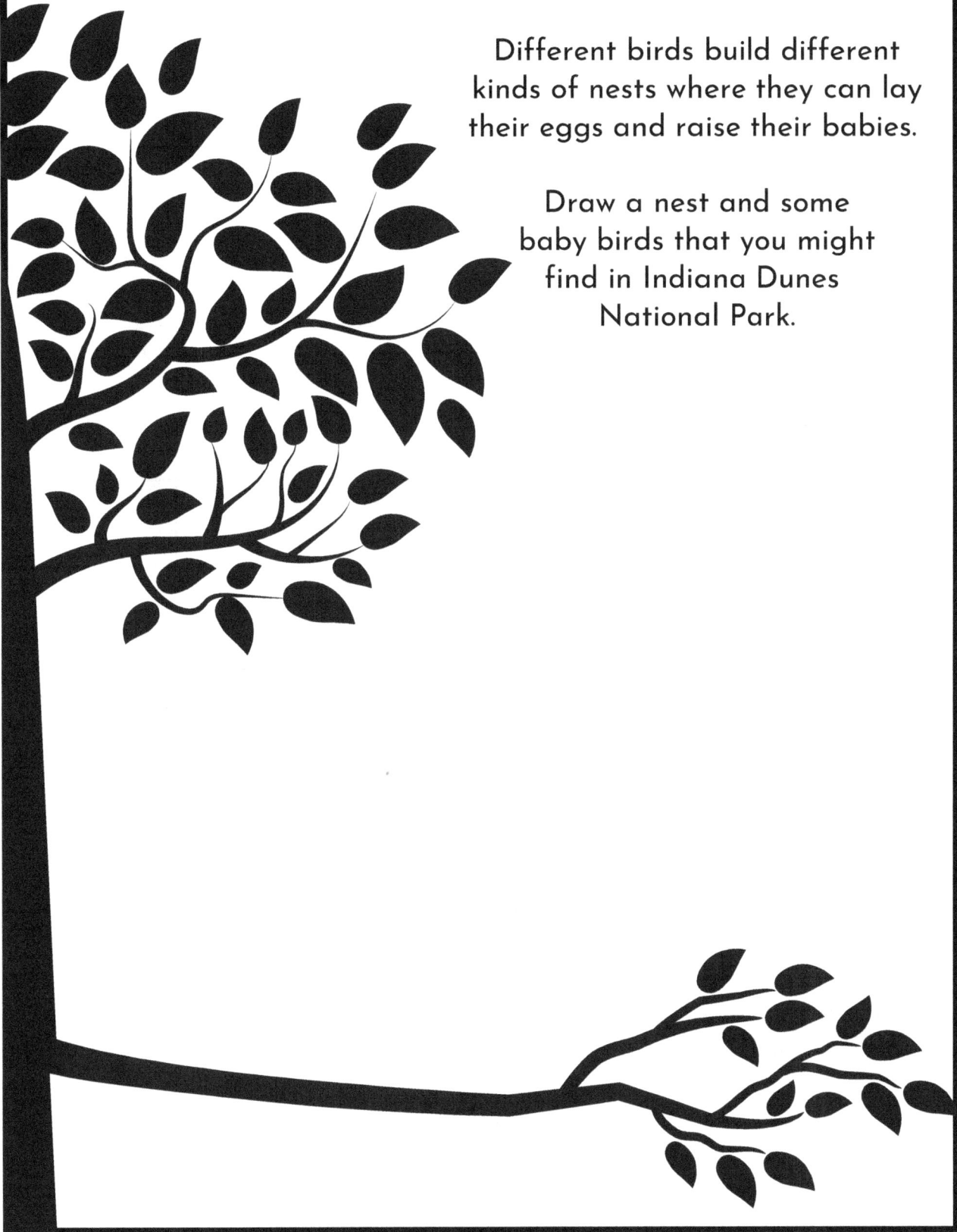

Go Birdwatching at Great Marsh Trail

start here →

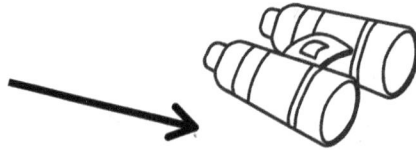

Camping Packing List

What should you take with you camping? Pretend you are in charge of your family camping trip. Make a list of what you would need to be safe and comfortable on an overnight excursion. Some considerations are listed on the side.

1.
2.
3.
4.
5.
6.
7.
8.
9.
10.
11.
12.
13.
14.
15.
16.

- What will you eat at every meal?

- What will the weather be like?

- Where will you sleep?

- What will you do during your free time?

- How luxurious do you want camp to be?

- How will you cook?

- How will you see at night?

- How will you dispose of trash?

- What might you need in case of emergencies?

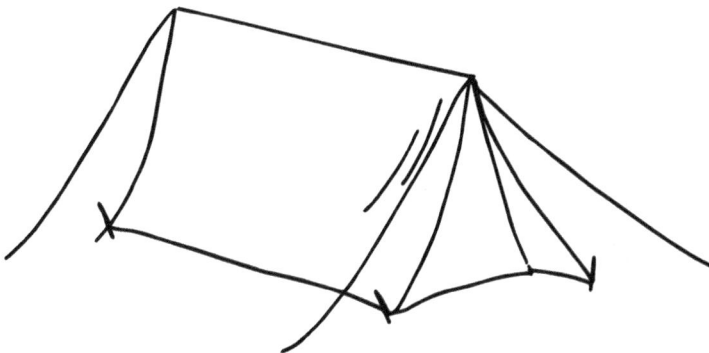

Indiana Dunes National Park

Date:

Season:

Who I went with:

Which entrance:

How was your experience? Write a few sentences on your trip. Where did you stay? What did you do? What was your favorite activity? If you have not yet visited the park, write a paragraph pretending that you did.

STAMPS

Many national parks and monuments have cancellation stamps for visitors to use. These rubber stamps record the date and the location that you visited. Many people collect the markings as a free souvenir. Check with a ranger to see where you can find a stamp during your visit. If you aren't able to find one, you can draw your own.

Where is the Park?

Indiana Dunes National Park is in the Midwest United States. It is located in Indiana, on the shores of Lake Michigan.

Indiana

Look at the shape of Indiana. Can you find it on the map? If you are from the US, can you find your home state? Color Indiana red. Put a star on the map where you live.

Connect the Dots #1

Connect the dots to figure out what this tiny critter is. One type of these live in Indiana Dunes National Park.

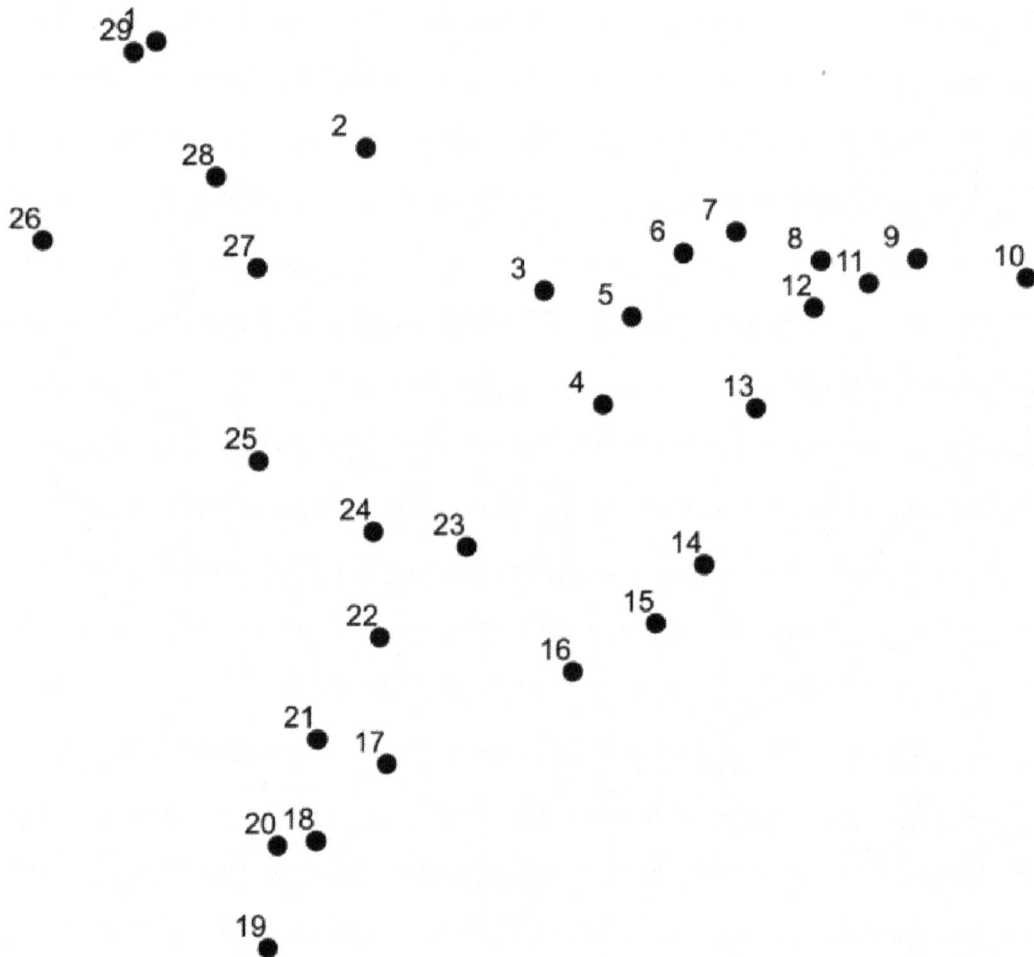

29
2
28
26
27
6 7
3 8 9 10
5 11
12
4 13
25
24 23
14
15
22
16
21 17
20 18
19

Their heart rate can reach as high as 1,260 beats per minute and a breathing rate of 250 breaths per minute. Have you ever measured your breathing rate? Ask a friend or family member to set a timer for 60 seconds. Once they say "go", try to breathe normally. Count each breath until they say "stop." How do your breaths per minute compare to hummingbirds?

_____

_____

While the Killdeer is technically a shorebird, you are more likely to find one in an open pasture or parking lot.

A skunk's sulfuric spray has a range of up to 10 feet, and its odor can be detected up to 1.5 miles.

Who lives here?

Here are eight plants and animals that live in the park.
Use the word bank to fill in the clues below.

WORD BANK: WILD YAM, MILKSNAKE, MINK, SUGAR MAPLE, SKUNK, BALD EAGLE, KILLDEER

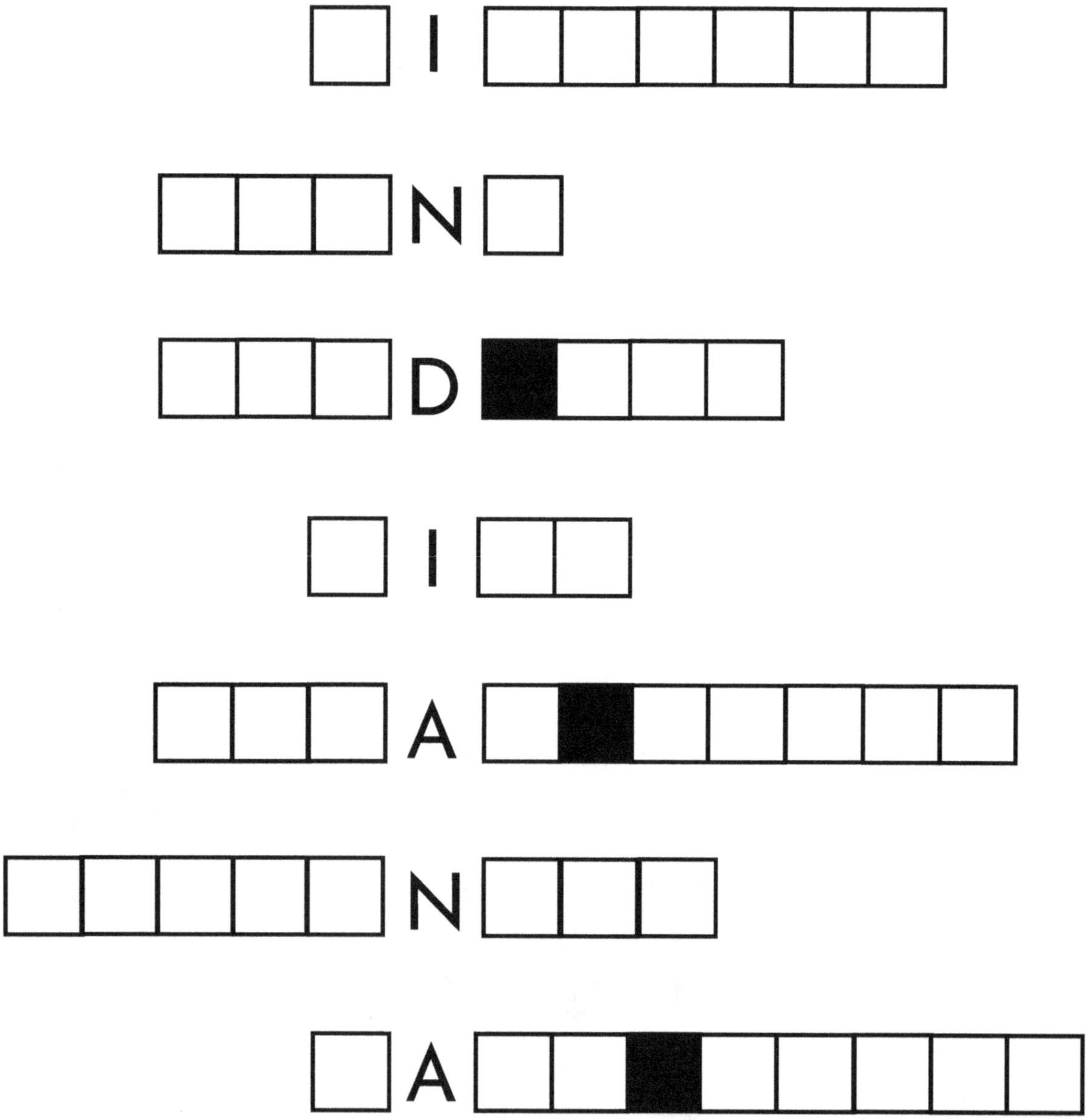

▢ I ▢ ▢ ▢ ▢ ▢

▢ ▢ ▢ N ▢

▢ ▢ ▢ D ■ ▢ ▢ ▢

▢ I ▢ ▢

▢ ▢ ▢ A ▢ ■ ▢ ▢ ▢ ▢ ▢

▢ ▢ ▢ ▢ ▢ N ▢ ▢

▢ A ▢ ▢ ■ ▢ ▢ ▢ ▢ ▢

Minks are highly active animals who can swim up to 100 feet underwater and jump from tree to tree.

The Milksnake is a species of kingsnake. Milksnakes are nonvenomous and harmless to humans.

Common Names
vs.
Scientific Names

A common name of an organism is a name that is based on everyday language. You have heard the common names of plants, animals, and other living things on tv, in books, and at school. Common names can also be referred to as "English" names, popular names, or farmer's name. Common names can vary from place to place. The word for a particular tree may be one thing, but that same tree has a different name in another country. Common names can even vary from region to region, even in the same country.

Scientific names, or Latin names, are given to organisms to make it possible to have uniform names for the same species. Scientific names are in Latin. You may have heard plants or animals referred to by their scientific name, or at least parts of their scientific names. Latin names are also called "binomial nomenclature" which refers to a two-part naming system. The first part of the name - the generic name -names the genus to which the species belongs. The second part of the name, the specific name, identifies the species. For example, Tyrannosaurus rex is an example of a widely known scientific name.

American Black Bear

Ursus americanus

COMMON NAME

Elk

Cervus canadensis

LATIN NAME = GENUS + SPECIES

Elk = Cervus canadensis

Black Bear = Ursus americanus

Find the Match!
Common Names and Latin Names

Match the common name to the scientific name for each animal. The first one is done for you. Use clues on the page before and after this one to complete the matches.

Red Fox	Haliaeetus leucocephalus
Black Oak	Taxidea taxus
Red Maple	Gavia pacifica
American Badger	Microtus ochrogaster
Great Horned Owl	Quercus velutina
Bald Eagle	Lampropeltis triangulum
Pacific Loon	Bubo virginianus
Prairie Vole	Vulpes vulpes
Eastern Milksnake	Acer rubrum

Red Fox

Vulpes vulpes

Pacific Loon
Gavia pacifica

Bald Eagle
Haliaeetus leucocephalus

Great Horned Owl
Bubo virginianus

Some plants and animals that live at the lakeshore.

Black Oak
Quercus velutina

American Badger
Taxidea taxus

Eastern Milksnake
Lampropeltis trianglulm

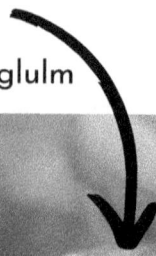

Making a Difference

It is important to protect the valuable resources of the world, not just beautiful places like national parks.

How many of these things do you do at home? If you answered "no" to more than 10 items, talk to the grownups in your life to see if there are any household habits you might be able to change. Conserving our collective resources helps us all.

Yes	No	Do you...
☐	☐	turn off the water when you are brushing your teeth?
☐	☐	use LED light bulbs when possible?
☐	☐	use a reusable water bottle instead of disposable ones?
☐	☐	ride your bike or take the bus instead of riding in the car?
☐	☐	have a rain barrel under your roof gutters to collect rain water?
☐	☐	take quick showers?
☐	☐	avoid putting more food on your plate than you will eat?
☐	☐	take reusable lunch containers?
☐	☐	grow a garden?
☐	☐	buy items with less packaging?
☐	☐	recycle paper?
☐	☐	recycle plastic?
☐	☐	have a compost pile at home so you can make your own soil?
☐	☐	pick up trash when you see it on the trail?
☐	☐	plan a "staycation" and fly only when you have to?

_____	_____
# of Yes	# of No

Add up your score! Are there any "no"s that you want to turn into a yes?

Can you think of any other ways to protect our natural resources?

_____

_____

The Ten Essentials

The ten essentials is a list of things that are important to have when you go for longer hikes. If you go on a hike to the <u>backcountry</u>, it is especially important that you have everything you need in case of an emergency. If you get lost or something unforeseen happens, it is good to be prepared to survive until help finds you.

The ten essentials list was developed in the 1930s by an outdoors group called the Mountaineers. Over time and technological advancements, this list has evolved. Can you identify all the things on the current list? Circle each of the "essentials" and cross out everything that doesn't make the cut.

fire: matches, lighter, tinder and/or stove	a pint of milk	extra money	headlamp plus extra batteries	extra clothes
extra water	a dog	Polaroid camera	bug net	lightweight games, like a deck of cards
extra food	a roll of duct tape	shelter	sun protection like sunglasses, sun-protective clothes and sunscreen	knife: plus a gear repair kit
a mirror	navigation: map, compass, altimeter, GPS device, or satellite messenger	first aid kit	extra flip-flops	entertainment like video games or books

Backcountry- a remote undeveloped rural area.

Rain, Rain, Rain

If it rains while you are visiting Indiana Dunes National Park, you can do this activity during your trip. If you don't get any rain while you are there, you can follow the same instructions next time it rains where you live.

Go outside into the rain. Use all of your senses as you complete the boxes below. You can use words, drawings, or both.

Sit as still as you can and listen to the rain. How does it make you feel?

Look straight up at the sky and let the raindrops fall on your face. Close your eyes. How does it feel?

Watch where the rain goes. Pay attention to the different surfaces the rain lands on. Which surfaces absorb the rain, and which surfaces cause the rain to run off or pool?

Are there any animals or bugs out enjoying the rain? Do you think the plants are enjoying the rain?

Connect the Dots #2

This animal lives in almost every state in the US, including the national park. They are nocturnal and are more active at night and sleep during the day. They are omnivorous eaters, which means they eat both plants and animals.

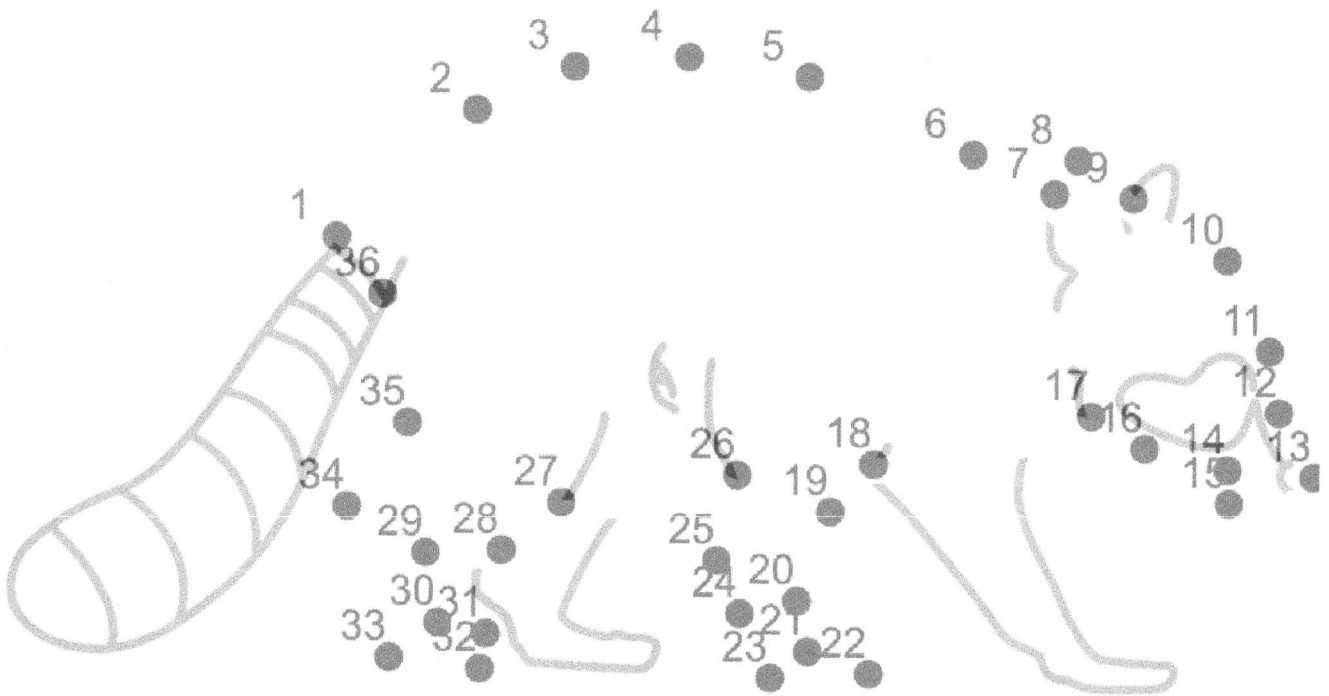

Are you an omnivore like a raccoon? An herbivore only eats plant foods. A carnivore only eats meat. An omnivore eats both. What type of eater are you? Write down some of your favorite foods to back up your answer.

_____

_____

LISTEN CAREFULLY

Visitors to Indiana Dunes National Park may hear different noises from those they hear at home. Try this activity to experience this for yourself!

First, find a place outside where it is comfortable to sit or stand for a few minutes. You can do this by yourself or with a friend or family member. Once you have a good spot, close your eyes and listen. Be quiet for one minute and pay attention to what you are hearing. List some of the sounds you have heard in one of the two boxes below:

NATURAL SOUNDS
MADE BY ANIMALS, TREES OR PLANTS, THE WIND, ETC

HUMAN-MADE SOUNDS
MADE BY PEOPLE, MACHINES, ETC

ONCE YOU ARE BACK AT HOME, TRY REPEATING YOUR EXPERIMENT:

NATURAL SOUNDS
MADE BY ANIMALS, TREES OR PLANTS, THE WIND, ETC

HUMAN-MADE SOUNDS
MADE BY PEOPLE, MACHINES, ETC

WHERE DID YOU HEAR MORE NATURAL SOUNDS? _____

WHERE DID YOU HEAR MORE HUMAN SOUNDS? _____

Indiana Dunes Bingo

Let's play bingo! Cross off each box that you are able to during your visit to the national park. Try to get a bingo down, across, or diagonally. If you can't visit the park, use the bingo board to plan your perfect trip.

Pick out some activities that you would want to do during your visit. What would you do first? How long would you spend there? What animals would you try to see?

SPOT A SALAMANDER	SEE A HERON	IDENTIFY A TREE	TAKE A PICTURE AT AN OVERLOOK	WATCH A MOVIE AT THE VISITORS CENTER
GO FOR A HIKE	LEARN ABOUT THE INDIGENOUS PEOPLE THAT LIVE IN THIS AREA	WITNESS A SUNRISE OR SUNSET	OBSERVE THE NIGHT SKIES	GO SWIMMING
HEAR A BIRD CALL	SPOT A BIG LAKE	FREE SPACE	LEARN ABOUT THE IMPORTANCE OF WETLANDS	VISIT A RANGER STATION
PICK UP TEN PIECES OF TRASH	GO CAMPING	SEE A WHITE-TAILED DEER	VISIT A BEACH	SPOT A BIRD OF PREY
LEARN ABOUT THE GEOLOGY OF THE DUNES	SEE SOMEONE RIDING A HORSE	HAVE A PICNIC	SPOT SOME ANIMAL TRACKS	PARTICIPATE IN A RANGER-LED ACTIVITY

Indiana Dunes Word Search

Words may be horizontal, vertical, or diagonal
and they might be backward!

1. Lake Michigan
2. sand
3. wetlands
4. ecology
5. hike
6. picnicking
7. orchids
8. birding
9. Mount Baldy
10. Little Calumet
11. fishing
12. camping
13. prairie
14. coyote
15. old-growth
16. Cowles Bog
17. biodiverse
18. foredunes
19. blowout dunes

```
L D E S F O R E D U N E S W C
C A M P I N G Z S W E R W R B
T V K N K G N I D R I B K O L
S E U E C O L O G Y U T B M O
H N N A M Q Y A L E Y R S K W
T P D L P I C N I C K I N G O
W E T O Y O C E R H W R L N U
O R B G E K I H I K E S V I T
R T H O I I L O I O T D E H D
G O I B R M O Y K G L G R S U
D S A S I C I C N L A B N I N
L H N E A A H I S A N N T F E
O J O L R H I I Z I D L W O S
E Y G W P I V E D N S A N D O
R B I O D I V E R S E O H E M
T T E C Y D L A B T N U O M T
U A E E S A E N N O A P V E B
C L I T T L E C A L U M E T N
```

25

Find the Match!
What are Baby Animals Called?

Match the animal to its baby. The first one is done for you.

Elk	eaglet
Bald Eagle	calf
Little Brown Bat	snakelets
Striped Skunk	pup
Great Horned Owl	owlet
Western Toad	kit
Mountain Lion	tadpole
Garter snake	kitten

Listen to the world around you...

Find a dry piece of ground free of animal poop. Lie on your back and shut your eyes. Make a fist. Every time you hear a sound, put on finger up. When you have 5 fingers up, make a list of all the things you heard.

_____

_____

_____

_____

_____

Review your list. Circle the sounds the belong in the wilderness. Put an X through the ones that don't.

Stop and smell the roses...

Use your nose! Find three things in the park that smell good and three that smell bad. List the things you smelled below.

Good

Bad

_____   _____

_____   _____

_____   _____

Review your list. Circle the sounds the belong in the wilderness. Put an X through the ones that don't.

The Perfect Picnic Spot

Fill in the blanks on this page without looking at the full story. Once you have each line filled out, use the words you've chosen to complete the story on the next page.

EMOTION_____

FOOD_____

SOMETHING SWEET_____

STORE_____

MODE OF TRANSPORTATION_____

NOUN_____

SOMETHING ALIVE_____

SAUCE_____

PLURAL VEGETABLES_____

ADJECTIVE_____

PLURAL BODY PART_____

ANIMAL_____

PLURAL FRUIT_____

PLACE_____

SOMETHING TALL_____

COLOR_____

ADJECTIVE_____

NOUN_____

A DIFFERENT ANIMAL_____

FAMILY MEMBER #1 _____

FAMILY MEMBER #2 _____

VERB THAT ENDS IN -ING _____

A DIFFERENT FOOD_____

The Perfect Picnic Spot

Use the words from the previous page to complete a silly story.

When my family suggested having our lunch at the Lake View Beach, I was

_____. I love eating my _____ outside! I knew we had picked up a
EMOTION   FOOD

box of _____ from the _____ for after lunch, my favorite. We drove up
SOMETHING SWEET STORE

to the area and I jumped out of the _____. "I will find the perfect spot for
          MODE OF TRANSPORTATION

a picnic!" I grabbed a _____ for us to sit on, and I ran off. I passed a picnic
      NOUN

table, but it was covered with _____ so we couldn't sit there. The next
       SOMETHING ALIVE

picnic table looked okay, but there were smears of _____ and pieces of
             SAUCE

_____ everywhere. The people that were there before must have been
PLURAL VEGETABLES

_____! I gritted my _____ together and kept walking down the path,
ADJECTIVE   PLURAL BODY PART

determined to find the perfect spot. I wanted a table with a good view of the

water. Why was this so hard? If we were lucky, I might even get to see _____
               ANIMAL

eating some _____ on the beach. They don't have those in _____ where I
   PLURAL FRUIT   PLACE

am from. I walked down a little hill and there it was, the perfect spot! The trees

towered overhead and looked as tall as _____. The patch of grass was a
       SOMETHING TALL

beautiful _____ color. The _____ flowers were growing on
   COLOR   ADJECTIVE

the side of a _____. I looked across the sandy beach and even saw a
    NOUN

_____ on the edge of a rock. I looked back to see my _____ and
DIFFERENT ANIMAL   FAMILY MEMBER #1

_____ _____ a picnic basket. "I hope you brought plenty of
FAMILY MEMBER #2 VERB THAT ENDS IN ING

_____, I'm starving!"
A DIFFERENT FOOD

29

Hike to Mount Baldy Beach

start here →

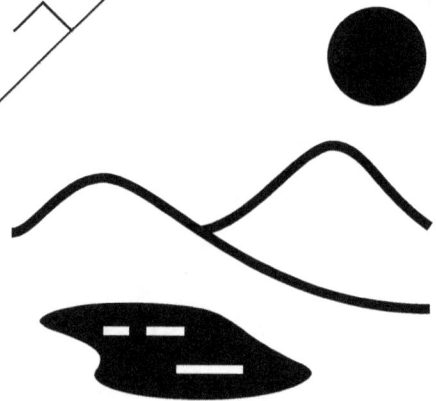

DID YOU KNOW?
Mount Baldy is moving 5-10 feet a year. Beach sand moves when the prevailing northwest wind blows at least 7 miles per hour.

Things to Find in the Dunes

Words may be horizontal, vertical, or diagonal
and they might be backward!

1. sand
2. footprints
3. driftwood
4. plant
5. shell
6. toad
7. dragonfly
8. lizard
9. wild grapes
10. rocks
11. gull
12. ladybug
13. goose
14. raccoon
15. trees
16. leaves
17. sticks

```
C W S L S P I R E S G U L L K
H T A S K I L D C H E L L N J
T F O O T P R I N T S B E P B
S M P A G A R S C E A L H C C
C E A D Z A B L D E N U S A L
A O L I S E P A R G D L I W I
R E L T E H E K A N K R I C N
P L B A M U I E G O O S E A G
R D R I F T W O O D I D Y D M
E C I C T B O Y N I P G O E A
Q T A N C H I N F R K E N S N
L E A V E S E I L A D Y B U G
I L O S H Z I S Y C C A L G T
P C G O L O K E S C O R V E R
N I C A K C I N T O A D H E E
X T T F O E E G L O E S Q N E
H Y D R O E L E C N R I C E S
C J S K C I T S N Y M A L A M
```

31

Leave No Trace Quiz

Leave No Trace is a concept that helps people make decisions during outdoor recreation that protects the environment. There are seven principles that guide us when we spend time outdoors, whether you are in a national park or not. Are you an expert in Leave No Trace? Take this quiz and find out!

1. How can you plan ahead and prepare to ensure you have the best experience you can in the national park?
   a. Make sure you stop by the ranger station for a map and to ask about current conditions.
   b. Just wing it! You will know the best trail when you see it.
   c. Stick to your plan, even if conditions change. You traveled a long way to get here, and you should stick to your plan.
2. What is an example of traveling on a durable surface?
   a. Walking only on the designated path.
   b. Walking on the grass that borders the trail if the trail is very muddy.
   c. Taking a shortcut if you can find one since it means you will be walking less.
3. Why should you dispose of waste properly?
   a. You don't need to. Park rangers love to pick up the trash you leave behind.
   b. You actually should leave your leftovers behind, because animals will eat them. It is important to make sure they aren't hungry.
   c. So that other peoples' experiences of the park are not impacted by you leaving your waste behind.
4. How can you best follow the concept "leave what you find"?
   a. Take only a small rock or leaf to remember your trip.
   b. Take pictures, but leave any physical items where they are.
   c. Leave everything you find, unless it may be rare like an arrowhead, then it is okay to take.
5. What is not a good example of minimizing campfire impacts?
   a. Only having a campfire in a pre-existing campfire ring.
   b. Checking in with current conditions when you consider making a campfire.
   c. Building a new campfire ring in a location that has a better view.
6. What is a poor example of respecting wildlife?
   a. Building squirrel houses out of rocks so the squirrels have a place to live.
   b. Stay far away from wildlife and give them plenty of space.
   c. Reminding your grown-ups to not drive too fast in animal habitats while visiting the park.
7. How can you show consideration of other visitors?
   a. Play music on your speaker so other people at the campground can enjoy it.
   b. Wear headphones on the trail if you choose to listen to music.
   c. Make sure to yell "Hello!" to every animal you see at top volume.

Park Poetry

America's parks inspire art of all kinds. Painters, sculptors, photographers, writers, and artists of all mediums have taken inspiration from natural beauty. They have turned their inspiration into great works.

Use this space to write your own poem about the park. Think about what you have experienced or seen. Use descriptive language to create an acrostic poem. This type of poem has the first letter of each line spell out another word. Create an acrostic that spells out the word "Dunes."

D _____

U _____

N _____

E _____

S _____

Delightful day
Unwinding
New adventures
Everyone at the beach
Sand in my toes

Diverse biology
Unique discoveries
Natvie plants
Exploring animals
So much to learn

Staying Safe in the Sun

It is important to take precautions to stay safe outdoors, especially when it is very hot outside. When someone gets overheated or dehydrated, they may feel sick or even require medical attention.

Use the cryptogram below to decode three tips on how to prevent heat-related illnesses. You may need to do some math to figure out the answers.

```
 T  __  __  __      __  __  __  __  __  __     __  __     __  __  __  __
12   5 12/2 50      30  21  50   5 2x3  36     3x4 27     21  50 6x6  12

 __  __     __  __  __     __  __  __  __  __ .
 99  10     15-3  4  50     36  7-3  5   1  50


 __  __  __  __         H  __  __  __  __  __  __  __                __  __
 36  12 1x5  18         4 2x9  1  21   5  12  50 8-7                 30  18

 __  __  __  __  __  __  __  __     __  __  __  __     __  __     __  __  __  __  __ .
  1  21  99  10   6 33x3 10  75     35 3x9  12  36     27 5x5    18/2  5  12  50  21


 __  __   A  __     __  __  __  __  __  __  __  __  __     __  __  __
  9  50 12-7 21     36   3  10  36  15  21 5x10 50  10      5  10 12-11

 __  __  __   -   __  __  __  __  __  __  __  __  __  __
 36   3  10       8  7x3 27  12  50  15 9+3  99  80  50

 __  __  __  __  __   I   N   G .
 15  35  27  12 2x2  99  10  75
```

a	b	c	d	e	f	g	h	i	j	k	l	m	n	o
5	30	15	1	50	25	75	4	99	20	6	35	49	10	27

p	q	r	s	t	u	v	w	x	y	z
8	16	21	36	12	3	80	9	40	18	7

Catch a Fish in the Little Calumet River

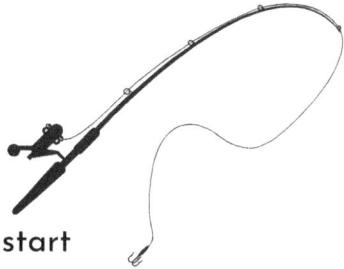

start here

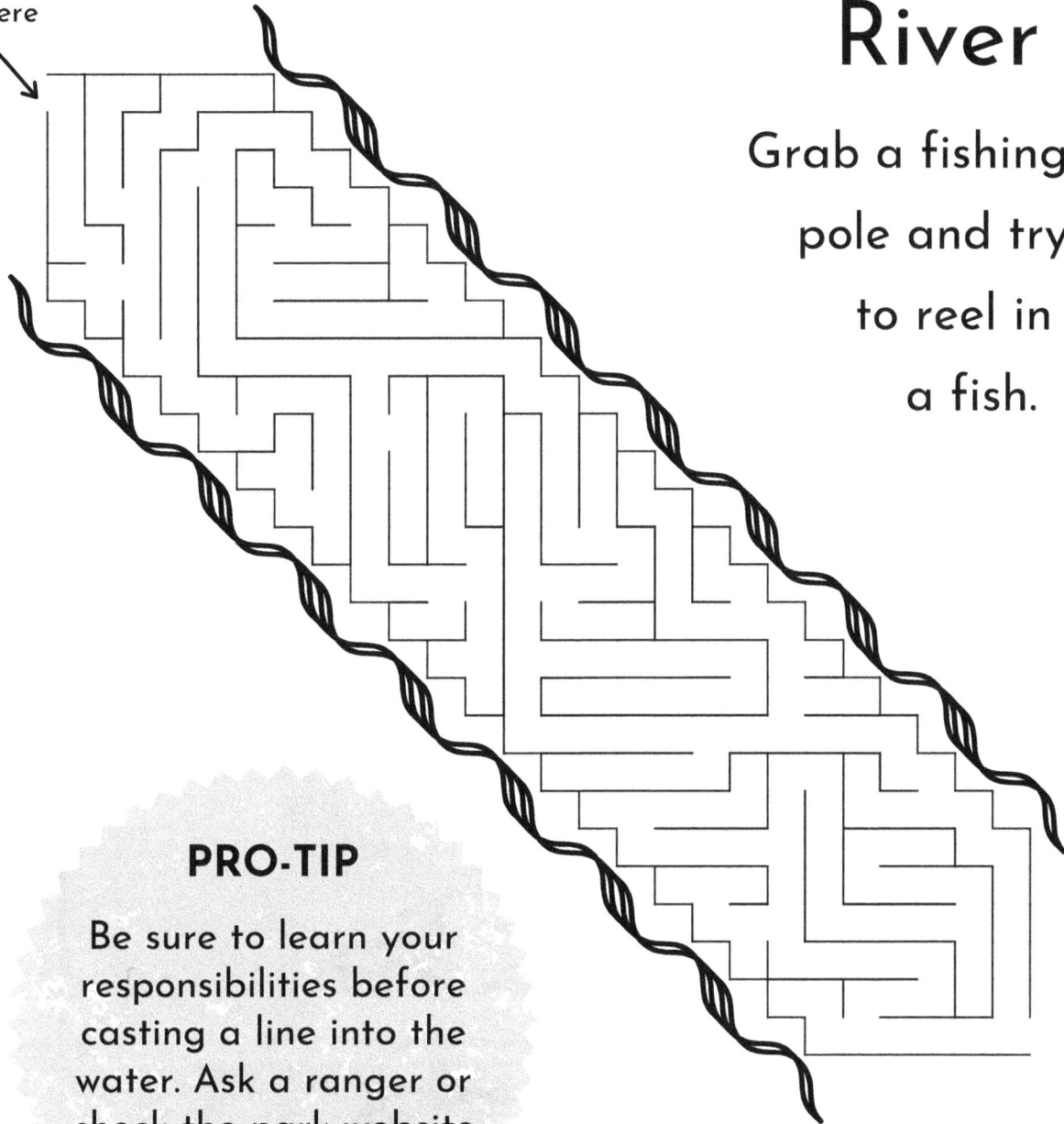

Grab a fishing pole and try to reel in a fish.

PRO-TIP

Be sure to learn your responsibilities before casting a line into the water. Ask a ranger or check the park website before you go.

Stacking Rocks

Have you ever seen stacks of rocks while hiking in national parks? Do you know what they are or what they mean? These rock piles are called cairns and often mark hiking routes in parks. Every park has a different way to maintain trails and cairns. However, they all have the same rule: If you come across a cairn, do not disturb it.

Color the cairn and the rules to remember.

1. Do not tamper with cairns.

If a cairn is tampered with or an unauthorized one is built, then future visitors may become disoriented or even lost.

2. Do not build unauthorized cairns.

Moving rocks disturbs the soil and makes the area more prone to erosion. Disturbing rocks can disturb fragile plants.

3. Do not add to existing cairns.

Authorized cairns are carefully designed. Adding to them can actually cause them to collapse.

Decoding Using American Sign Language

American Sign Language, also called ASL for short, is a language that many Deaf people or people who are hard of hearing use to communicate. People use ASL to communicate with their hands. Did you know people from all over the country and world travel to national parks? You may hear people speaking other languages. You might also see people using ASL. Use the American Manual Alphabet chart to decode some national parks facts.

This was the first national park to be established:

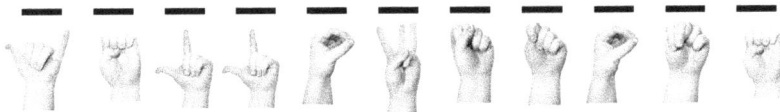

This is the biggest national park in the US:

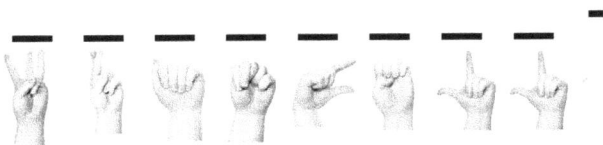

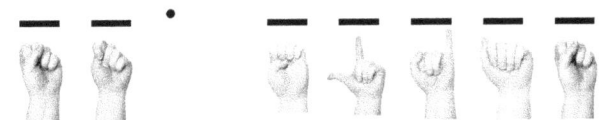

This is the most visited national park:

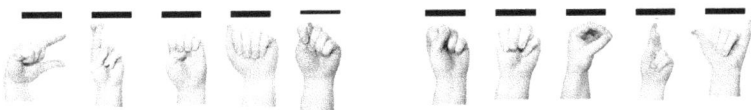

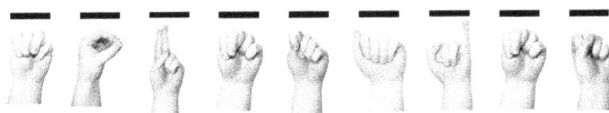

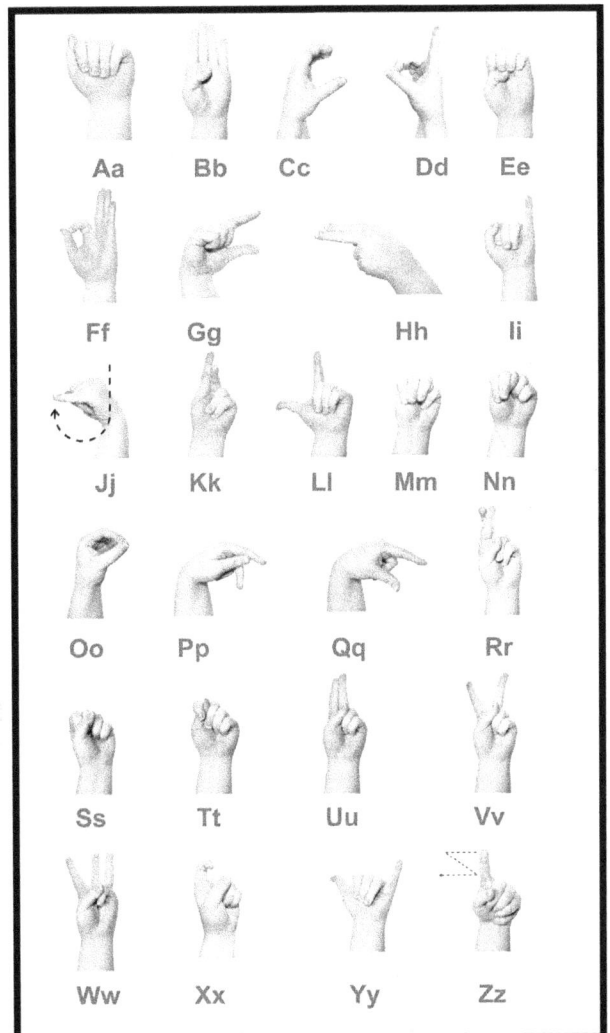

Aa	Bb	Cc	Dd	Ee
Ff	Gg		Hh	Ii
Jj	Kk	Ll	Mm	Nn
Oo	Pp		Qq	Rr
Ss	Tt		Uu	Vv
Ww	Xx		Yy	Zz

Hint: Pay close attention to the position of the thumb!

Try it! Using the chart, try to make the letters of the alphabet with your hand. What is the hardest letter to make? Can you spell out your name? Show a friend or family member and have them watch you spell out the name of the national park you are in.

Go Horseback Riding on the Glenwood Dunes Trails

Help find the horse's lost shoe!

start
here

DID YOU KNOW?

Horseback riding is a popular activity in Indiana Dunes National Park. There are many trails that you can take horses for day or overnight trips.

Butterflies of Indiana Dunes

Over sixty species of butterflies and moths live in Indiana Dunes National Park. Their wingspan size varies, as do the patterns on their wings. Design your own butterfly below. Make sure the wings are symmetrical, meaning both sides match.

A Hike at Cowles Bog

Fill in the blanks on this page without looking at the full story. Once you have each line filled out, use the words you've chosen to complete the story on the next page.

ADJECTIVE _____

SOMETHING TO EAT _____

SOMETHING TO DRINK _____

NOUN _____

ARTICLE OF CLOTHING _____

BODY PART _____

VERB _____

ANIMAL _____

SAME TYPE OF FOOD _____

ADJECTIVE _____

SAME ANIMAL _____

VERB THAT ENDS IN "ED" _____

NUMBER _____

A DIFFERENT NUMBER _____

SOMETHING THAT FLIES _____

LIGHT SOURCE _____

PLURAL NOUN _____

FAMILY MEMBER _____

YOUR NICKNAME _____

A Hike at Cowles Bog

Use the words from the previous page to complete a silly story.

I went for a hike at Cowles Bog today. In my favorite _ _ _ _ _ _ _ backpack, I
ADJECTIVE

made sure to pack a map so I wouldn't get lost. I also threw in an extra

_ _ _ _ _ _ _ _ _ _ _ just in case I got hungry and a bottle of _ _ _ _ _ _ _ _ _ _. I put
SOMETHING TO EAT   SOMETHING TO DRINK

on my _ _ _ _ _ _ _ _ _ spray, and a tied a _ _ _ _ _ _ _ _ _ _ _ _ around my
NOUN   ARTICLE OF CLOTHING

_ _ _ _ _ _ _ _ _ _, in case it gets chilly. I started to _ _ _ _ _ _ down the path. As
BODY PART   VERB

soon as I turned the corner, I came face to face with a(n) _ _ _ _ _ _ _ _. I think
ANIMAL

it was as startled as I was! What should I do? I had to think fast! Should I

give it some of my _ _ _ _ _ _ _ _ _ _ _? No. I had to remember what the
SAME TYPE OF FOOD

_ _ _ _ _ _ _ ranger told me. "If you see one, back away slowly and try not to
ADJECTIVE

scare it." Soon enough, the _ _ _ _ _ _ _ _ _ _ _ _ _ _ _ _ _ _ _ _ away. The coast
SAME ANIMAL   VERB THAT ENDS IN ED

was clear. _ _ _ _ _ _ hours later, I finally got to the lookout. I felt like I could
NUMBER

see for a _ _ _ _ _ _ miles. I took a picture of a _ _ _ _ _ _ _ _ so I could always
A DIFFERENT NUMBER   NOUN

remember this moment. As I was putting my camera away, a _ _ _ _ _ _ _ _ _
SOMETHING THAT FLIES

flew by, reminding me that it was almost nighttime. I turned on my

_ _ _ _ _ _ _ _ _ _ and headed back. I could hear the _ _ _ _ _ _ _ _ _ _ singing their
LIGHT SOURCE   PLURAL INSECT

evening song. Just as I was getting tired, I saw my _ _ _ _ _ _ _ _ _ and our tent.
FAMILY MEMBER

"Welcome back _ _ _ _ _ _ _ _! How was your hike?"
NICKNAME

Design a Badge

Imagine you've been hired to create a badge that will be for sale in the national park gift shop. Your badge will be a souvenir for visitors to remember their trip to the park.

Consider adding a plant or animal that lives here, or include a famous place in the park or activity that you can do while visiting.

Let's Go Camping
Word Search

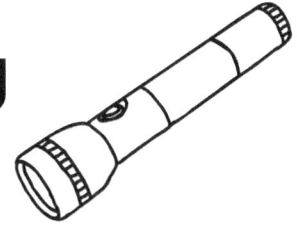

Words may be horizontal, vertical, or diagonal and they might be backward!

1. tent
2. camp stove
3. sleeping bag
4. bug spray
5. sunscreen
6. map
7. flashlight
8. pillow
9. lantern
10. ice
11. snacks
12. smores
13. water
14. first aid kit
15. chair
16. cards
17. books
18. games
19. trail
20. hat

```
D P P I L L O W D B T E A C I
E O A D P R E A A M B R C A N
P W C A M P S T O V E I H X G
R A H S G E L E B E E D A P S
E L B U G S P R A Y N G I E A
S I A H G C I C N N M E R C N
C W N L A F I R S K O O B F K
M T A E M I L E L H M R W L J
T A P R E A O R E S L B A A B
S M P A S R R T E N T L U S C
C E A I I R C G P E I U J H A
S S N A C K S S I M O K I L R
I J R S F O I S N J R A Q I D
C Y E T L E V E G U O R V G S
E W T A K C A B B S S O H H M
X J N F I R S T A I D K I T T
U A A E S S E N G E T P V A B
C J L I A R T D N A M A H A S
```

43

All in the Day of a Park Ranger

Park Rangers are hardworking individuals dedicated to protecting our parks, monuments, museums, and more. They take care of the natural and cultural resources for future generations. Rangers also help protect the visitors of the park. Their responsibilities are broad and they work both with the public and behind the scenes.

What have you seen park rangers do? Use your knowledge of the duties of park rangers to fill out a typical daily schedule, one activity for each hour. Feel free to make up your own, but some examples of activities are provided on the right. Read carefully, not all of the example activities are befitting a ranger!

6 am	Lead a sunrise hike
7 am	
8 am	
9 am	
10 am	
11 am	
12 pm	Enjoy a lunch break outside
1 pm	
2 pm	
3 pm	
4 pm	Teach visitors about the geology of the dunes
5 pm	
6 pm	
7 pm	
8 pm	
9 pm	

- feed the bald eagles
- build trails for visitors to enjoy
- throw rocks off the side of the dunes
- rescue lost hikers
- study animal behavior
- record air quality data
- answer questions at the visitor center
- pick wildflowers
- pick up litter
- share marshmallows with squirrels
- repair handrails
- lead a class on a field trip
- catch frogs and make them race
- lead people on educational hikes
- write articles for the park website
- protect the lake from pollution
- remove non-native plants from the park
- study how climate change is affecting the park
- give a talk about mountain lions
- lead a program for campers on fish

If you were a park ranger, which of the above tasks would you enjoy most?

_____

44 _____

Draw Yourself as a Park Ranger

RANGER

The Fish of Indiana Dunes

1.

NINWOM

Unscramble these common fish names that live in the park.

2.

OTRTU

3.

LASNOM

4.

SPINLUC

5.

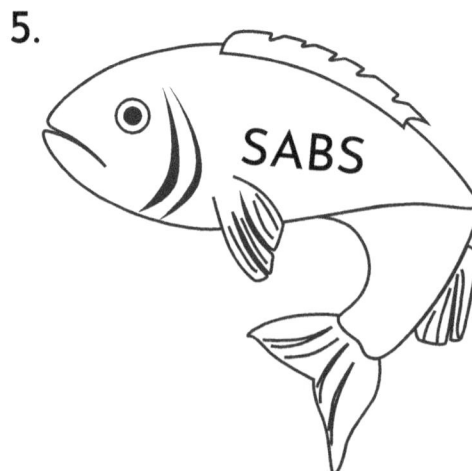

SABS

1. _____

2. _____

3. _____

4. _____

5. _____

Word Bank

salmon
sunfish
trout
minnow
sculpin
bass
whitefish
catfish

Amphibians

Two species of toad and eight species of frogs live in Indiana Dunes National Park. Even more types of salamanders live there too. Frogs and toads both spend the beginning of their lives the same way, as tadpoles. Tadpoles hatch from eggs in water, usually in springs or pools of water.

Both frogs and toads are amphibians. Salamanders are amphibians too. Color the amphibians below.

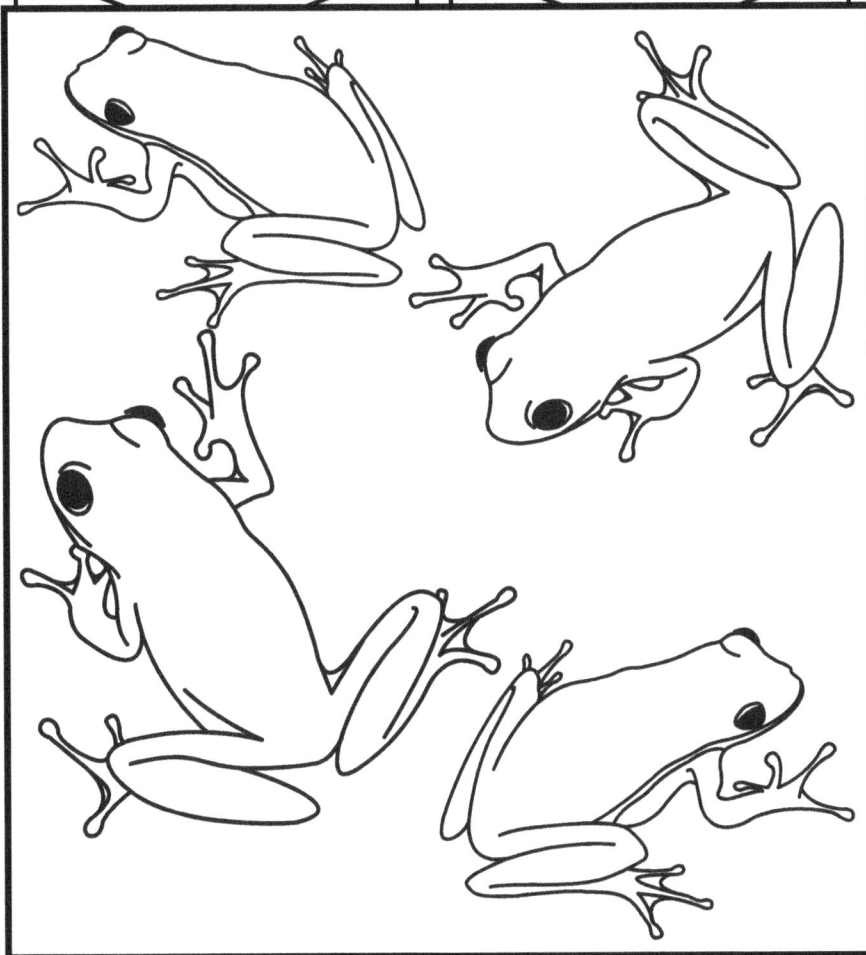

The National Park Logo

The National Park System has over 400 units in the US. Just like Indiana Dunes National Park, each location is unique or special in some way. The areas include other national parks, historic sites, monuments, seashores, and other recreation areas.

Each element of the National Park emblem represents something that the National Park Service protects. Fill in each blank below to show what each symbol represents.

```
WORD BANK:
MOUNTAINS, ARROWHEAD, BISON,
SEQUOIA TREE, WATER
```

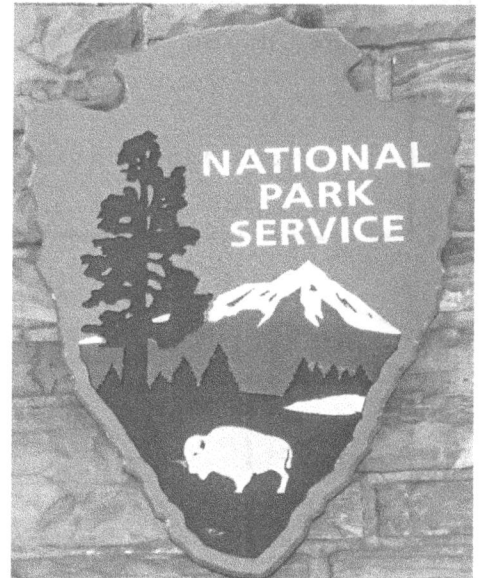

This represents all plants. _____

This represents all animals. _____

This symbol represents the landscapes. _____

This represents the waters protected by the park service. _____

This represents the historical and archeological values. _____

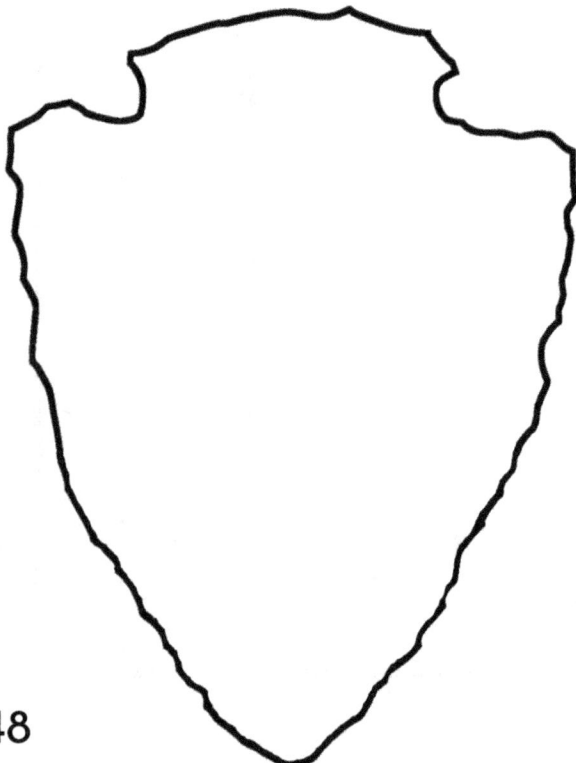

Now it's your turn! Pretend you are designing a new national park. Add elements to the design that represent the things that your park protects

What is the name of your park?

Describe why you included the symbols that you included. What do they mean?

Weather Watch

Find a place where you are in an open area where you can easily see the sky. Complete the activities below to provide your weather report. If you aren't in the park, you can do this activity from home.

Can you feel any wind?

What does the sky look like?

Is there anything you notice about the weather today?

What is the date?

What is the time?

Where is the sun in the sky? (rising, midpoint, falling)

What direction is the wind blowing?

Are there clouds in the sky? If so, draw them below:

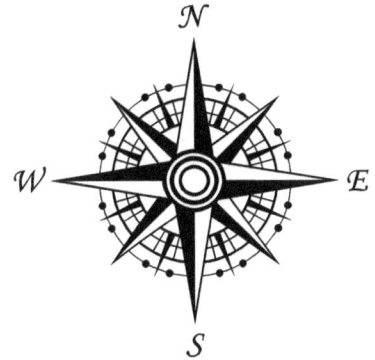

63 National Parks

How many other national parks have you been to? Which one do you want to visit next? Note that some of these parks fall on the border of more than one state, you may check it off more than once!

Alaska
- [ ] Denali National Park
- [ ] Gates of the Arctic National Park
- [ ] Glacier Bay National Park
- [ ] Katmai National Park
- [ ] Kenai Fjords National Park
- [ ] Kobuk Valley National Park
- [ ] Lake Clark National Park
- [ ] Wrangell-St. Elias National Park

American Samoa
- [ ] National Park of American Samoa

Arizona
- [ ] Grand Canyon National Park
- [ ] Petrified Forest National Park
- [ ] Saguaro National Park

Arkansas
- [ ] Hot Springs National Park

California
- [ ] Channel Islands National Park
- [ ] Death Valley National Park
- [ ] Joshua Tree National Park
- [ ] Kings Canyon National Park
- [ ] Lassen Volcanic National Park
- [ ] Pinnacles National Park
- [ ] Redwood National Park
- [ ] Sequoia National Park
- [ ] Yosemite National Park

Colorado
- [ ] Black Canyon of the Gunnison National Park
- [ ] Great Sand Dunes National Park
- [ ] Mesa Verde National Park
- [ ] Rocky Mountain National Park

Florida
- [ ] Biscayne National Park
- [ ] Dry Tortugas National Park
- [ ] Everglades National Park

Hawaii
- [ ] Haleakala National Park
- [ ] Hawai'i Volcanoes National Park

Idaho
- [ ] Yellowstone National Park

Kentucky
- [ ] Mammoth Cave National Park

Indiana
- [ ] Indiana Dunes National Park

Maine
- [ ] Acadia National Park

Michigan
- [ ] Isle Royale National Park

Minnesota
- [ ] Voyageurs National Park

Missouri
- [ ] Gateway Arch National Park

Montana
- [ ] Glacier National Park
- [ ] Yellowstone National Park

Nevada
- [ ] Death Valley National Park
- [ ] Great Basin National Park

New Mexico
- [ ] Carlsbad Caverns National Park
- [ ] White Sands National Park

North Dakota
- [ ] Theodore Roosevelt National Park

North Carolina
- [ ] Great Smoky Mountains National Park

Ohio
- [ ] Cuyahoga Valley National Park

Oregon
- [ ] Crater Lake National Park

South Carolina
- [ ] Congaree National Park

South Dakota
- [ ] Badlands National Park
- [ ] Wind Cave National Park

Tennessee
- [ ] Great Smoky Mountains National Park

Texas
- [ ] Big Bend National Park
- [ ] Guadalupe Mountains National Park

Utah
- [ ] Arches National Park
- [ ] Bryce Canyon National Park
- [ ] Canyonlands National Park
- [ ] Capitol Reef National Park
- [ ] Zion National Park

Virgin Islands
- [ ] Virgin Islands National Park

Virginia
- [ ] Shenandoah National Park

Washington
- [ ] Mount Rainier National Park
- [ ] North Cascades National Park
- [ ] Olympic National Park

West Virginia
- [ ] New River Gorge National Park

Wyoming
- [ ] Grand Teton National Park
- [ ] Yellowstone National Park

Other National Parks

Besides Indiana Dunes National Park, there are 62 other diverse and beautiful national parks across the United States. Try your hand at this crossword. If you need help, look at the previous page for some hints.

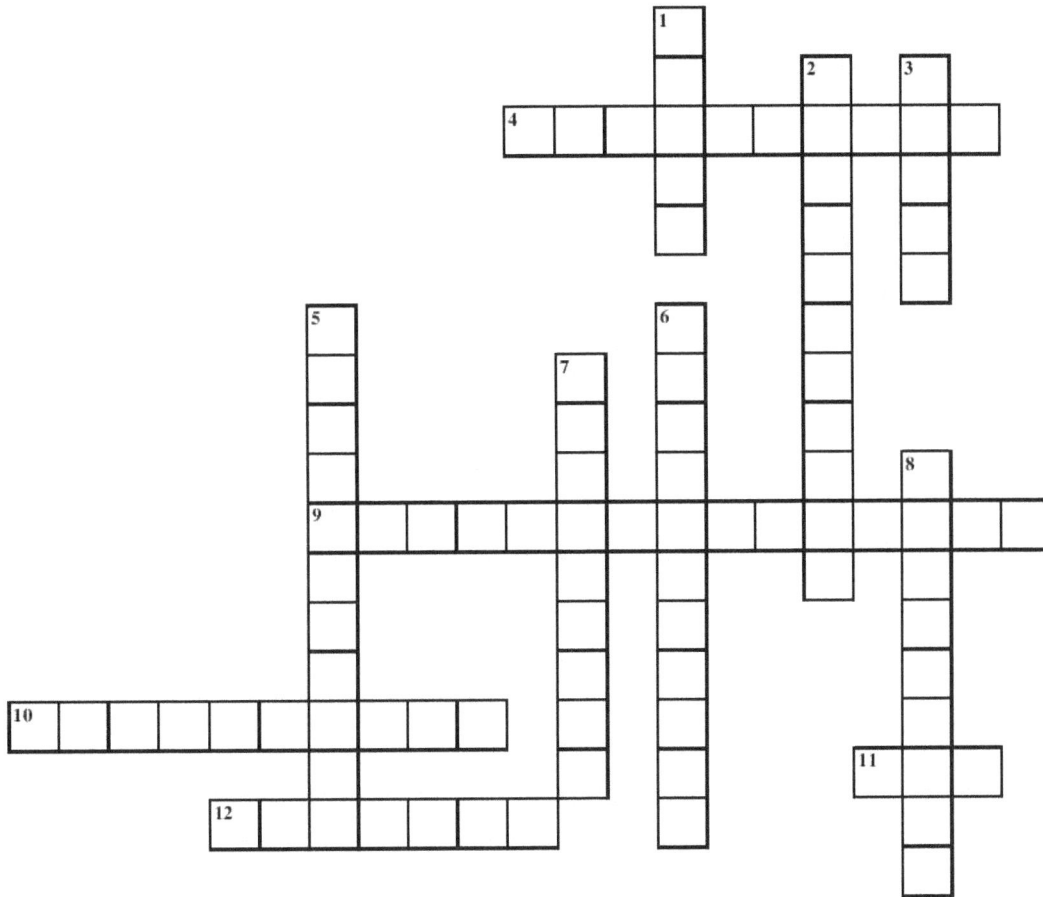

Down

1. State where Acadia National Park is located
2. This national park has the Spanish word for turtle in it.
3. Number of national parks in Alaska
5. This national park has some of the hottest temperatures in the world.
6. This national park is the only one in Idaho.
7. This toothsome creature can be famously found in Everglades National Park.
8. Only president with a national park named for them

Across

4. This state has the most national parks.
9. This park has some of the newest land in the US, caused by volcanic eruptions.
10. This park has the deepest lake in the United States.
11. This color shows up in the name of a national park in California.
12. This national park deserves a gold medal.

Which National Park Will You Go to Next?
Word Search

1. Zion
2. Big Bend
3. Glacier
4. Olympic
5. Sequoia
6. Bryce
7. Mesa Verde
8. Biscayne
9. Wind Cave
10. Great Basin
11. Katmai
12. Yellowstone
13. Voyageurs
14. Arches
15. Badlands
16. Denali
17. Glacier Bay
18. Hot Springs

```
F M M E S A V E R D E B N E Y
E A B I G B E N D E S A S E M
Y L I C A L O Y N E E D L T G
D M G A S S A U C N R L U E R
C E L I I T S C R E O A A K E
S N A W Y E E O I W T N A C A
G I C H A A Q C S E M D N S T
N O I Z P R U T I M R S N E B
I W E L M P O N B W E B K H A
R J R F D N I F L I H B U C S
P A B E E S A N E S O P W R I
S J A E N Y A C S I B A U A N
T C Y I A D O H H Y M E A L R
O T A T L M L E S E G R W R J
H S T O I K A T M A I R O P B
I C H U R C O L Y M P I C O U
O Y G T S D E O S B R Y C E T
W I N D C A V E I N R O H E M
```

Field Notes

Spend some time to reflect on your trip to Indiana Dunes National Park. Your field notes will help you remember the things you experienced. Use the space below to write about your day.

While I was at Indiana Dunes National Park...

I saw:

_____

_____

_____

_____

_____

I heard:

_____

_____

_____

_____

I felt:

_____

_____

Draw a picture of your favorite thing in the park.

_____

_____

I wondered:

_____

_____

_____

_____

_____

_____

ANSWER KEY

National Park Emblem Answers

1. This represents all plants. **Sequoia Tree**

2. This represents all animals. **Bison**

3. This symbol represents the landscapes. **Mountains**

4. This represents the waters protected by the park service. **Water**

5. This represents the historical and archeological values. **Arrowhead**

Jumbles Answers

1. BOATING

2. HIKING

3. BIRDING

4. CAMPING

5. PICNICKING

6. SIGHTSEEING

7. STAR GAZING

Go Birdwatching at Great Marsh Trail

start here

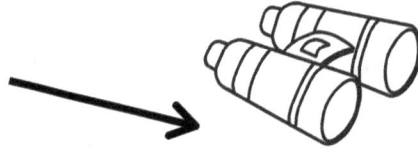

DID YOU KNOW?
Indiana Dunes
National Park is home
to several birds of
prey, including eagles,
hawks, and owls. Birds
of prey are birds that
hunt other animals for
food.

Answers: Who lives here?

Here are eight plants and animals that live in the park.
Use the word bank to fill in the clues below.

WORD BANK: WILD YAM, MILKSNAKE, MINK, SUGAR MAPLE, SKUNK, BALD EAGLE, KILLDEER

K I LLDEER

SKU N K

WIL D ▪ YAM

M I NK

SUG A R ▪ MAPLE

MILKS N AKE

B A LD ▪ EAGLE

Find the Match!
Common Names and Latin Names

Match the common name to the scientific name for each animal. The first one is done for you. Use clues on the page before and after this one to complete the matches.

Red Fox — Haliaeetus leucocephalus

Black Oak — Taxidea taxus

Red Maple — Gavia pacifica

American Badger — Microtus ochrogaster

Great Horned Owl — Quercus velutina

Bald Eagle — Lampropeltis triangulum

Pacific Loon — Bubo virginianus

Prairie Vole — Vulpes vulpes

Eastern Milkshake — Acer rubrum

Bald Eagle

Haliaeetus leucocephalus

Answers: The Ten Essentials

The ten essentials is a list of things that are important to have when you go for longer hikes. If you go on a hike to the <u>backcountry</u>, it is especially important that you have everything you need in case of an emergency. If you get lost or something unforeseen happens, it is good to be prepared to survive until help finds you.

The ten essentials list was developed in the 1930s by an outdoors group called the Mountaineers. Over time and technological advancements, this list has evolved. Can you identify all the things on the current list? Circle each of the "essentials" and cross out everything that doesn't make the cut.

(fire: matches, lighter, tinder and/or stove) ⭕	a pint of milk ❌	extra money ❌	(headlamp plus extra batteries) ⭕	(extra clothes) ⭕
(extra water) ⭕	a dog ❌	Polaroid camera ❌	bug net ❌	lightweight games like a deck of cards ❌
(extra food) ⭕	a roll of duct tape ❌	(shelter) ⭕	(sun protection like sunglasses, sun-protective clothes and sunscreen) ⭕	(knife: plus a gear repair kit) ⭕
a mirror ❌	(navigation: map, compass, altimeter, GPS device, or satellite messenger) ⭕	(first aid kit) ⭕	extra flip-flops ❌	entertainment like video games or books ❌

Backcountry- a remote undeveloped rural area.

Things to Find in the Dunes

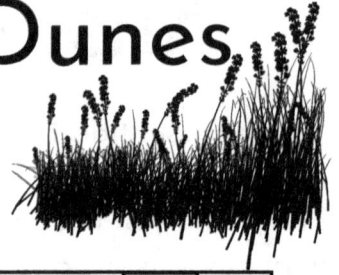

Words may be horizontal, vertical, or diagonal
and they might be backward!

1. sand
2. footprints
3. driftwood
4. plant
5. shell
6. toad
7. dragonfly
8. lizard
9. wild grapes
10. rocks
11. gull
12. ladybug
13. goose
14. raccoon
15. trees
16. leaves
17. sticks

```
C W S L S P I R E S G U L L K
H T A S K I L D C H E L L N J
T F O O T P R I N T S B E P B
S M P A G A R S C E A L H C C
C E A D Z A B L D E N U S A L
A O L I S E P A R G D L I W I
R E L T E H E K A N K R I C N
P L B A M U I E G O O S E A G
R D R I F T W O O D I D Y D M
E C I C T B O Y N I P G O E A
Q T A N C H I N F R K E N S N
L E A V E S E I L A D Y B U G
I L O S H Z I S Y C C A L G T
P C G O L O K E S C O R V E R
N I C A K C I N T O A D H E E
X T T F O E E G L O E S Q N E
H Y D R O E L E C N R I C E S
C J S K C I T S N Y M A L A M
```

60

Answers: Find the Match! What are Baby Animals Called?

Match the animal to its baby. The first one is done for you.

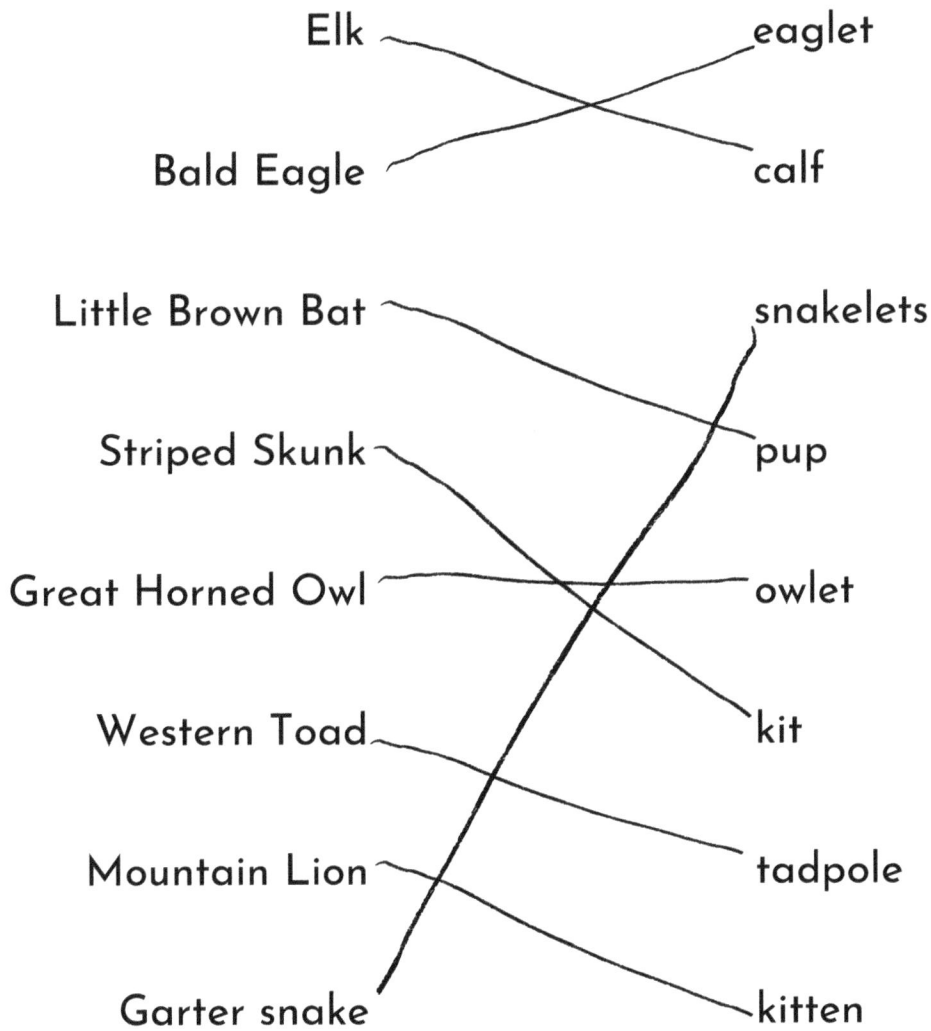

Elk — eaglet

Bald Eagle — calf

Little Brown Bat — snakelets

Striped Skunk — pup

Great Horned Owl — owlet

Western Toad — kit

Mountain Lion — tadpole

Garter snake — kitten

Solution: Hike to Mount Baldy Beach

DID YOU KNOW?
Mount Baldy is moving 5-10 feet a year. Beach sand moves when the prevailing northwest wind blow at least 7 miles per hour.

Indiana Dunes Word Search

Words may be horizontal, vertical, or diagonal
and they might be backward!

1. Lake Michigan
2. sand
3. wetlands
4. ecology
5. hike
6. picnicking
7. orchids
8. birding
9. Mount Baldy
10. Little Calumet
11. fishing
12. camping
13. prairie
14. coyote
15. old-growth
16. Cowles Bog
17. biodiverse
18. foredunes
19. blowout dunes

```
L D E S F O R E D U N E S W C
C A M P I N G Z S W E R W R B
T V K N K G N I D R I B K O L
S E U E C O L O G Y U T B M O
H N N A M Q Y A L E Y R S K W
T P D L P I C N I C K I N G O
W E T O Y O C E R H W R L N U
O R B G E K I H I K E S V I T
R T H O I I L O I O T D E H D
G O I B R M O Y K G L G R S U
D S A S I C I C N L A B N I N
L H N E A A H I S A N N T F E
O J O L R H I I Z I D L W O S
E Y G W P I V E D N S A N D O
R B I O D I V E R S E O H E M
T T E C Y D L A B T N U O M T
U A E E S A E N N O A P V E B
C L I T T L E C A L U M E T N
```

63

Answers: Leave No Trace Quiz

Leave No Trace is a concept that helps people make decisions during outdoor recreation that protects the environment. There are seven principles that guide us when we spend time outdoors, whether you are in a national park or not. Are you an expert in Leave No Trace? Take this quiz and find out!

1. How can you plan ahead and prepare to ensure you have the best experience you can in the National Park?

   A. Make sure you stop by the ranger station for a map and to ask about current conditions.

2. What is an example of traveling on a durable surface?

   A. Walking only on the designated path.

3. Why should you dispose of waste properly?

   C. So that other peoples' experiences of the park are not impacted by you leaving your waste behind.

4. How can you best follow the concept "leave what you find"?

   B. Take pictures but leave any physical items where they are.

5. What is not a good example of minimizing campfire impacts?

   C. Building a new campfire ring in a location that has a better view.

6. What is a poor example of respecting wildlife?

   A. Building squirrel houses out of rocks from the river so the squirrels have a place to live.

7. How can you show consideration of other visitors?

   B. Wear headphones on the trail if you choose to listen to music.

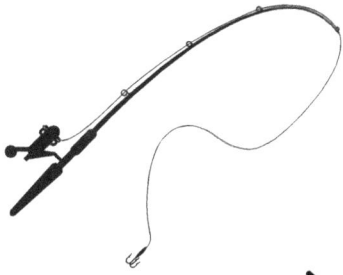

Solution: Catch a Fish in the Little Calumet River

Grab a fishing pole and try to reel in a fish.

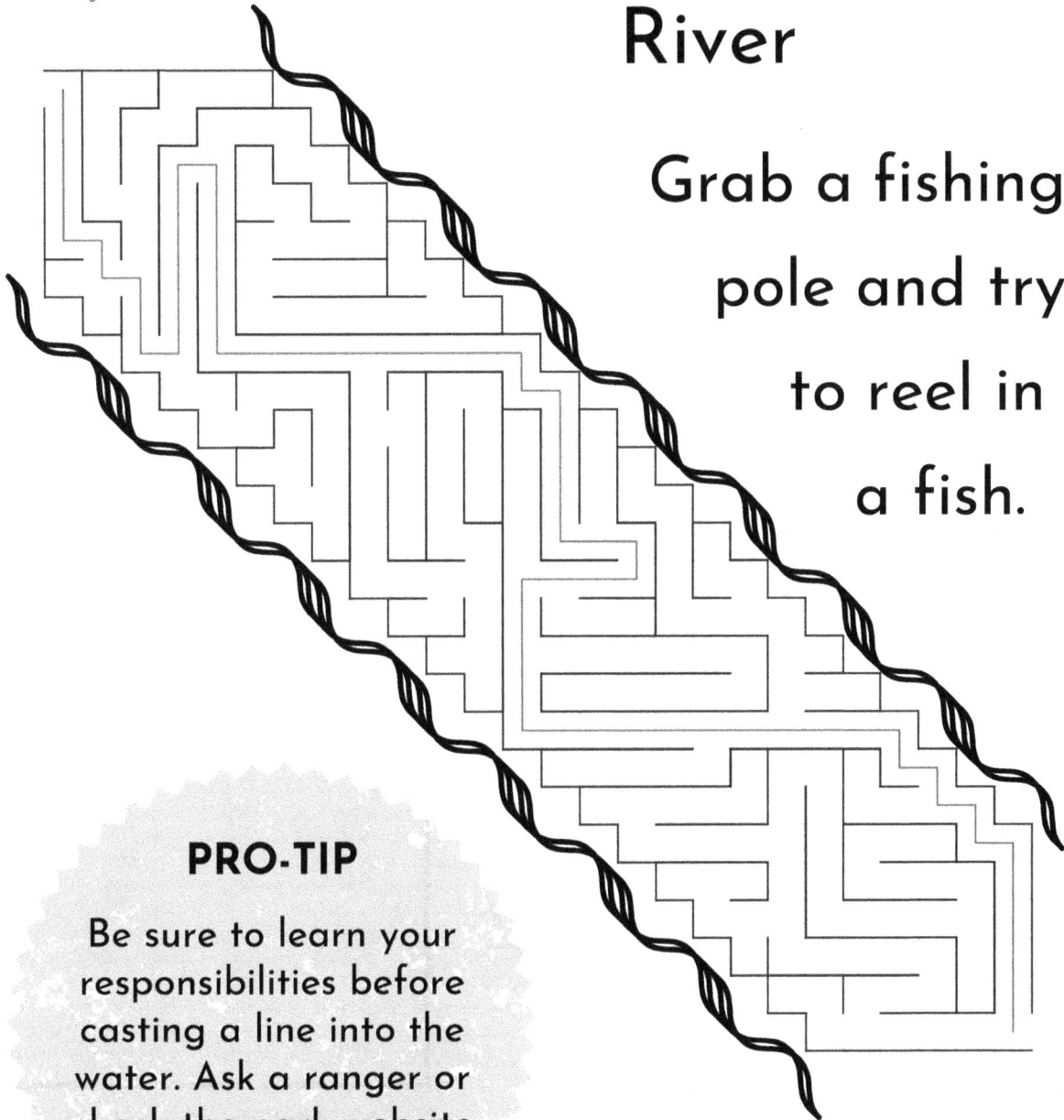

PRO-TIP

Be sure to learn your responsibilities before casting a line into the water. Ask a ranger or check the park website before you go.

Decoding Using American Sign Language

American Sign Language, also called ASL for short, is a language that many Deaf people or people who are hard of hearing use to communicate. People use ASL to communicate with their hands. Did you know people from all over the country and world travel to national parks? You may hear people speaking other languages. You might also see people using ASL. Use the American Manual Alphabet chart to decode some national parks facts.

This was the first national park to be established:

Y E L L O W S T O N E

This is the biggest national park in the US:

W R A N G E L L -

S T .   E L I A S

This is the most visited national park:

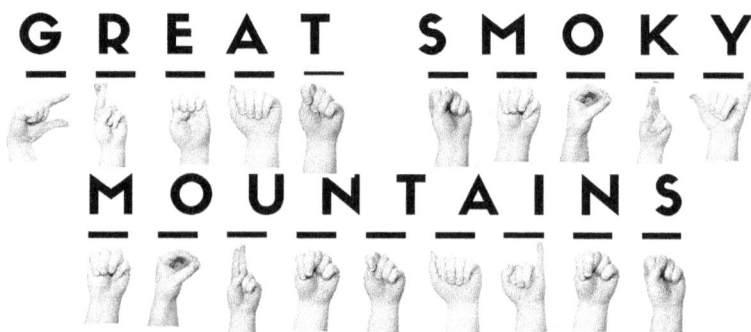

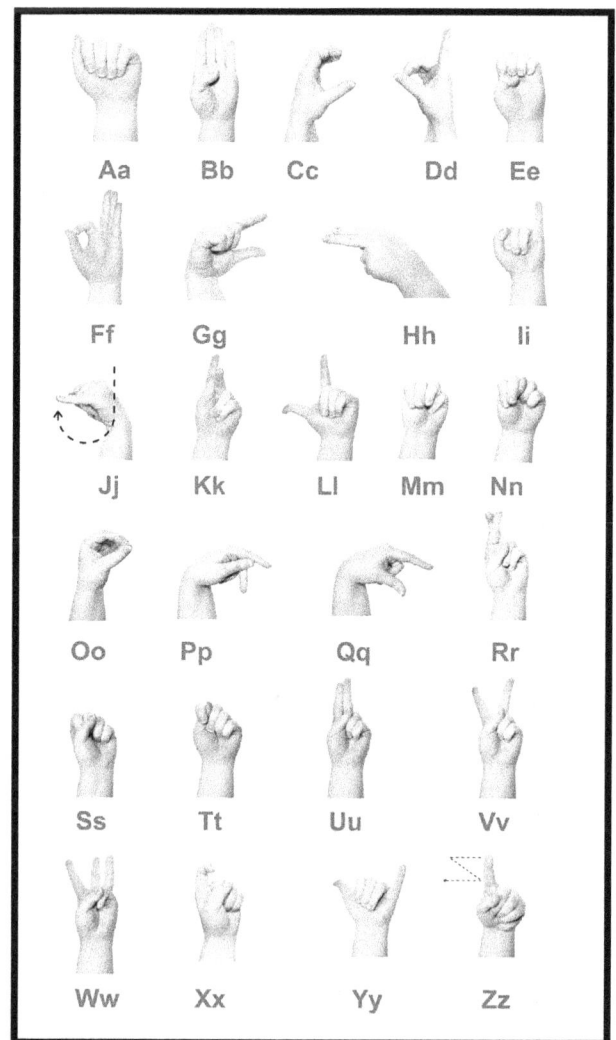

G R E A T   S M O K Y

M O U N T A I N S

Aa	Bb	Cc	Dd	Ee
Ff	Gg		Hh	Ii
Jj	Kk	Ll	Mm	Nn
Oo	Pp		Qq	Rr
Ss	Tt	Uu	Vv	
Ww	Xx	Yy	Zz	

Hint: Pay close attention to the position of the thumb!

Try it! Using the chart, try to make the letters of the alphabet with your hand. What is the hardest letter to make? Can you spell out your name? Show a friend or family member and have them watch you spell out the name of the national park you are in.

Go Horseback Riding on the Glenwood Dunes Trails

Help find the horse's lost shoe!

start here

DID YOU KNOW?

Horseback riding is a popular activity in Indiana Dunes National Park. There are many trails that you can take horses for day or overnight trips.

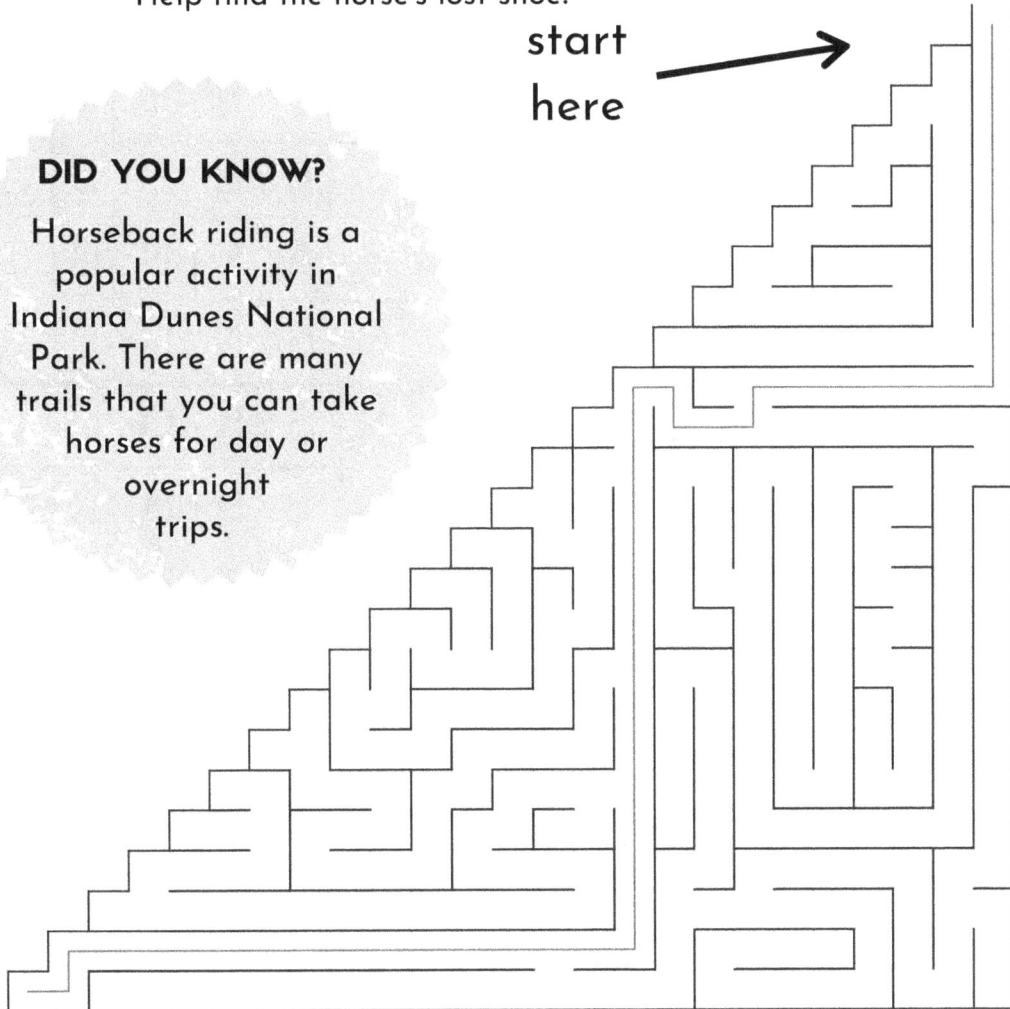

Let's Go Camping
Word Search

1. tent
2. camp stove
3. sleeping bag
4. bug spray
5. sunscreen
6. map
7. flashlight
8. pillow
9. lantern
10. ice
11. snacks
12. smores
13. water
14. first aid kit
15. chair
16. cards
17. books
18. games
19. trail
20. hat

```
D P P I L L O W D B T E A C I
E O A D P R E A A M B R C A N
P W C A M P S T O V E I H X G
R A H S G E L E B E E D A P S
E L B U G S P R A Y N G I E A
S I A H G C I C N N M E R C N
C W N L A F I R S K O O B F K
M T A E M I L E L H M R W L J
T A P R E A O R E S L B A A B
S M P A S R R T E N T L U S C
C E A I I R C G P E I U J H A
S S N A C K S S I M O K I L R
I J R S F O I S N J R A Q I D
C Y E T L E V E G U O R V G S
E W T A K C A B B S S O H H M
X J N F I R S T A I D K I T T
U A A E S S E N G E T P V A B
C J L I A R T D N A M A H A S
```

Fish of Indiana Dunes

1.
NINWOM

2.
OTRTU

Unscramble these common fish names that live in the park.

3.
LASNOM

4.
SPINLUC

1. <u>MINNOW</u>
2. <u>TROUT</u>
3. <u>SALMON</u>
4. <u>SCULPIN</u>
5. <u>BASS</u>

5.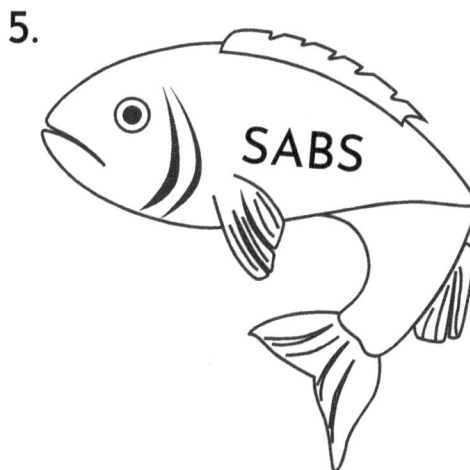
SABS

Word Bank

salmon
sunfish
trout
minnow
sculpin
bass
whitefish
catfish

Answers: Other National Parks

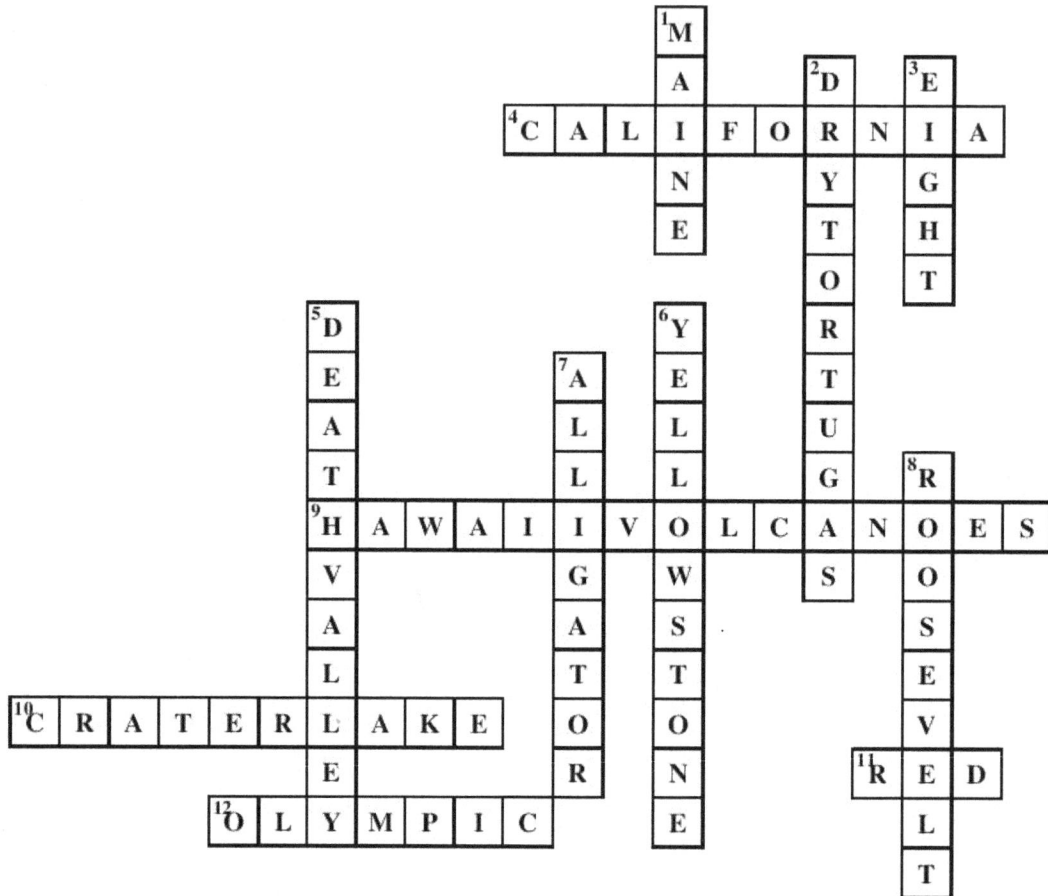

```
              ¹M
              A         ²D      ³E
      ⁴C A L I F O R N I A
              N         Y       G
              E         T       H
                        O       T
      ⁵D              ⁶Y        R
      E         ⁷A    E         T
      A         L     L         U
      T         L     L     ⁸R
      ⁹H A W A I I V O L C A N O E S
      V         G     W     A   O
      A         A     S     S   S
      L         T     T         E
   ¹⁰C R A T E R L A K E        V
      E         O     O     ¹¹R E D
      ¹²O L Y M P I C  N         L
                     E          T
```

Down	Across
1. State where Acadia National Park is located	4. This state has the most National Parks
2. This National Park has the Spanish word for turtle in it	9. This park has some of the newest land in the US, caused by a volcanic eruption
3. Number of National Parks in Alaska	10. This park has the deepest lake in the United States
5. This National Park has some of the hottest temperatures in the world	11. This color shows up in the name of a National Park in California
6. This National Park is the only one in Idaho	12. This National Park deserves a gold medal
7. This toothsome creature can be famously found in Everglades National Park	
8. Only president with a national park named for them	

Answers: Where National Park Will You Go Next?

1. Zion
2. Big Bend
3. Glacier
4. Olympic
5. Sequoia
6. Bryce
7. Mesa Verde
8. Biscayne
9. Wind Cave
10. Great Basin
11. Katmai
12. Yellowstone
13. Voyageurs
14. Arches
15. Badlands
16. Denali
17. Glacier Bay
18. Hot Springs

F M M E S A V E R D E B N E Y
E A B I G B E N D E S A S E M
Y L I C A L O Y N E E D L T G
D M G A S S A U C N R L U E R
C E L I I T S C R E O A A K E
S N A W Y E E O I W T N A C A
G I C H A A Q C S E M D N S T
N O I Z P R U T I M R S N E B
I W E L M P O N B W E B K H A
R J R F D N I F L I H B U C S
P A B E E S A N E S O P W R I
S J A E N Y A C S I B A U A N
T C Y I A D O H H Y M E A L R
O T A T L M L E S E G R W R J
H S T O I K A T M A I R O P B
I C H U R C O L Y M P I C O U
O Y G T S D E O S B R Y C E T
W I N D C A V E I N R O H E M